West Coast Birds

WEST COAST BIRDS

Chris C. Fisher

LONE
PINE

The Publisher
Lone Pine Publishing

206, 10426–81 Avenue	202A, 1110 Seymour St.	16149 Redmond Way, #180
Edmonton, Alberta	Vancouver, BC	Redmond, Washington
Canada T6E 1X5	Canada V6B 3N3	U.S.A. 98052

Canadian Cataloguing in Publication Data
Fisher, Chris, 1970–
   West Coast birds

Includes index.
ISBN 1-55105-049-8

1. Birds—British Columbia—Pacific Coast—Identification. 2. Birds—Northwest, Pacific—Identification. 3. Bird watching—British Columbia—Pacific Coast. 4. Bird watching—Northwest, Pacific. 5. Large type books. I. Title.
QL685.5.B8F57 1996   598.29711'1   C95-911235-9

Senior Editor: *Nancy Foulds*
Editors: *Jennifer Keane, Roland Lines*
Design & Layout: *Bruce Timothy Keith, Greg Brown, Carol S. Dragich*
Colour Illustrations: *Gary Ross, Ewa Pluciennik, Joan Johnston,*
         Kitty Ho, Beata Kurpinski
Cover Illustration: *Gary Ross*
Separations and Film: *Elite Lithographers Co. Ltd., Edmonton, Alberta*
Printing: *Quebecor Jasper Printing, Edmonton, Alberta*

The Publisher gratefully acknowledges the support of Alberta Community Development, the Department of Canadian Heritage and the Canada/Alberta Agreement on the cultural industries.

Acknowledgments

A book such as this is made possible by the inspired work of west coast naturalists past and present. Their contributions continue to advance the science of ornithology and to motivate a new generation of nature lovers. My thanks to Gary Ross and Ewa Pluciennik, whose illustrations have elevated the quality of this book well beyond the written medium. To Carole Patterson for her constant support, and to Robin Bovey, Bryan Gates, and especially Wayne Campbell, whose previous works served as models of excellence. Many thanks to the team at Lone Pine Publishing—Shane Kennedy, Jennifer Keane, Roland Lines, and Nancy Foulds—for their input and steering. Finally, my sincere thanks to Jim Butler for his encouragement, and to Nancy Baron and John Acorn for their comments, direction, and influence.

Contents
Intro   8

Black Songbirds   69
Crows, Ravens, Starlings

Mid-sized Birds   74
Thrushes, Jays, Kingfishers

Woodpeckers   83

Small Showy Birds   87
Chickadees, Swallows, Warblers

Small Brown Birds   100
Sparrows, Wrens, Flycatchers

Introduction

No matter where we live, birds are a natural part of our lives. We are so used to seeing them that we often take their presence for granted. When we take the time to notice their colours, songs, and behaviours, we see how dynamic these creatures are.

This book presents a brief introduction into the lives of birds. It is intended to serve as a bird identification guide, and also as a bird appreciation guide. Getting to know a bird's name is the first step toward getting to know birds. Once we've made contact with a species, we can better appreciate its character and mannerisms during future encounters. When we know a bit about them, their songs will sound sweeter, their plumage will look brighter, and their hardships will no longer be discounted out of ignorance. Over a lifetime of meetings, many birds become acquaintances, some seen daily, others not for years.

The selection of species within this book represents a balance between the familiar and the noteworthy. Many of the 91 species described in this guide are the most common species found along the west coast; some are less common. It would be impossible for an introductory book such as this to comprehensively describe all the birds found along the Pacific

Coast from Northern California to the Alaskan Panhandle. The birds' natural abundance and distribution patterns ensure that their populations vary considerably from place to place. There is no one site where all the species within this book can be observed simultaneously, but most species can be viewed—at least seasonally—within a few hours' drive (or sail) of most cities and towns.

The real story of birds unfolds outdoors. It is hoped that this guide will inspire novice birdwatchers into spending some time outdoors, gaining valuable experience with the local bird community. Unfortunately, many people who desire those personal experiences find it very difficult to venture into the natural kingdom. This book stresses the identity of birds, but it also attempts to bring them to life by discussing their various character traits. We often discuss a bird's character traits in human terms, because personifying a bird's character can help us to feel a bond with the birds. These associations contribute greatly to our introduc-tion to birds, but it is vital to realize that when we personify the actions of birds we satisfy our imaginations, but we do not do justice to their complex behavior.

Birding 'by Ear'

Sometimes, bird listening can be more effective than birdwatching. The technique of birding by ear is gaining popularity, because listening for birds can be more efficient, productive and rewarding than waiting for a visual confirmation. Birds have distinctive songs for resolving territorial disputes, and therefore sound is an effective way to identify species. It is particularly effective when trying to watch some of the smaller forest-dwelling birds. Their size and often indistinct plumage can make a visual search of the forest canopy frustrating. To facilitate auditory searches, catchy paraphrases are included in the descriptions of many of the songbirds in this book. Many excellent CDs and tapes are available at bookstores and wild bird stores for the songs of the birds in your area.

The Organization of This Book

Most other field guides are directed toward accomplished birdwatchers who are capable of sorting out which of the 800 species occur in their region, in strict phylogenic order. There is nothing wrong with many of these excellent guides, but they are very complex. Novice birdwatchers rarely have the five-or ten-minute view of a species that is required to search those large volumes. *West Coast Birds* groups birds by physical appearance and behaviour, without adhering to the scientific criterion for bird classification. It is easier for a novice to associate a wren as a 'small brown bird' than as a 'Troglodytidae.' It is hoped that this simplified order will allow you to spend more time with the birds and less time fumbling through a field guide.

Surface Birds
Loons, Grebes, Cormorants

This large, diverse group of waterbirds is most frequently seen swimming and diving on the surface of coastal waters. They are also seen flying over the sea, and are (with a few easily identified exceptions) infrequently seen on land. There is much overlap in physical similarity between this group and the sea birds and waterfowl; all sections should be looked over for uncertain species.

Waterfowl
Swans, Geese, Ducks

Because there are so many waterbirds on the coast, we decided to group the duck family together. This family includes the swans, geese, and ducks, most of which have a characteristic spoon-shaped bill. They are seen on land and on coastal and inland water. The sea ducks and mergansers may associate with birds in the surface bird category, but their size and physical features allow them to stand out.

Sea Birds
Alcids, Gulls, Terns

Alcids are stocky, stubby winged birds usually seen on the ocean or rocky shorelines. Gulls and terns are widespread; they are light-coloured and are graceful fliers.

Long-legged Birds
Herons, Sandpipers, Plovers

Many of these birds are seen in close proximity to the coastal shoreline, either wading in the water or scurrying along the shore. Their legs are long and slender, providing an easy identification feature.

Birds of Prey
Hawks, Eagles, Owls

Birds of this group are identified by their powerful talons and bills, and their forward-facing eyes. They prey almost exclusively on other animals.

Game Birds
Grouse, Quail

The three species in this group resemble domestic poultry and are best identified by their stocky bodies and short, low flights. They are usually seen on the ground.

Black Songbirds
Crows, Ravens, Starlings

These unrelated birds all share jet-black plumage. It is important to realize that although all the birds in this group are black, they do not all belong to the Blackbird family.

Mid-sized Birds
Thrushes, Jays, Kingfishers

The birds within this group are all about the size of a robin. Many have distinctive songs and plumage, helping in their identification.

Woodpeckers

The drumming sound of drilling wood and these birds' precarious foraging habits easily identify most members of this distinctive group.

Small Showy Birds
Chickadees, Swallows, Warblers

These birds are grouped together on the basis of size and colour. All are smaller than a robin and have bold plumages of more than one dominant color.

Small Brown Birds
Sparrows, Wrens, Flycatchers

The small, indistinct birds are predominantly brown or olive. Their songs are often very useful in identification.

Seasons of Birdwatching

Spring

Although spring on the west coast may appear to arrive gradually, birdwatchers will notice a sudden change in season. Ducks and geese migrating north concentrate on ponds and estuaries, and leave with many of the overwintering species. Loons, grebes, and shorebirds molt into their exquisite breeding attire and leave the coast for their inland breeding spots. From the south, swallows and warblers return to fill the fields and forests with activity. Owls and songbirds fill the nights and days with song.

Spring is the best time of year to watch birds. Deciduous trees have not yet sprouted the leaves that birds enjoy hiding behind, and love-sick male birds are often exceptionally bold.

Summer

The breeding time of birds comes all too quickly for birdwatchers. Summertime finds birds busy with their nesting, and less likely to put on shows for human observers. Singing decreases in favour of nest-building and incubation. Once the chicks are born, the parent(s) are kept busy feeding the insatiable young.

For fortunate west coast residents with occupied nest boxes in their yards, summer can be extremely enjoyable. Watching the birds' reproductive cycles, from breeding to fledging, can provide some memorable experiences. Summer closes with the youngs' first clumsy flight of the year.

Autumn

The great fall migration along the west coast is an opportunity to observe rare and unexpected species. Birds breeding in Siberia often take a wrong turn at the Bering Strait and follow our coastline south, much to the delight of west coast birdwatchers. The misguided birds complement the hordes of migrants that flood onto the west coast from breeding grounds on the prairies and in the Arctic. Although many birds have lost the magnificence of their spring plumage, a good fall day at a west coast estuary may reveal tens of thousands of birds.

Winter

Birds knew long before humans that for its latitude, a west coast winter can't be surpassed. Backyard

feeders do good business during the coldest parts of the year because natural food items require greater effort. Overwintering birds are found everywhere—offshore and in wetlands, woodlands, and city parks. Although their behaviours are not as elaborate as they are in the spring, many enjoyable winter afternoons can be spent watching rafts of water birds foraging on the choppy sea.

Habitat

Knowing where you are looking often reduces the confusion of what you are looking at. Because you won't find a loon up a tree or a grouse out at sea, habitat is an important thing to note when birdwatching.

The quality of habitat is one of the most powerful factors to influence bird distribution, and with experience you may become amazed by the predictability of some birds within a specific habitat type. Coastal water turns up predictable species seasonally. Scoters and guillemots can frequently be seen in the Pacific, but are unlikely to venture inland. Likewise, a cormorant seen inland is quite likely a Double-crested, while a coastal cormorant will require a second or third look to identify it.

Shorelines, of course, are the spot for shorebirds, but different varieties will occur in different areas. Exposed mudflats will attract Dunlin and Plovers, while rocky shorelines are almost never without at least one pair of Black Oystercatchers. Look for the birds you expect to see in the habitat where you are.

Open areas such as farms and fields boast a whole different community of birds. Swallows and sparrows can be common there, along with Northern Harriers and Red-tailed Hawks. Northwestern Crows, Starlings, and Rock Doves are found in city parks, but not in the same bushy areas as Chickadees, Wrens and Bushtits. Although these associations may now appear complex, they can be extremely useful. Just as humans are seldom seen away from our built-up environment, so birds are confined to environments that grant them a sense of security.

Habitat Icons

Each bird in this guide is accompanied by at least one habitat symbol that represents a general environment where the bird is most likely to be seen. These habitat categories will work in most situations, but vagrants and migrating birds can turn up in just about any habitat type. These unexpected surprises are among the most powerful motivations for the increasing legion of birdwatchers.

Coast

Wetlands

Forests

Fields and Pastures

Garden Feeders

Manicured
Residential Parks

West Coast Birds

Common Loon
(*Gavia immer*)

When ice locks northern lakes, thousands of Common Loons retreat to coastal waters to spend the winter months. Their intricate dark green and white wardrobe gives way to winter browns, and Common Loons quiet the spirited, mournful songs that invigorate and sanctify their summer homes.

The Common Loon that visits the west coast may be more subdued, but this bird is common in name alone. The loon is a noble symbol of northern wilderness, preferring the diminishing pristine areas where birds alone quarrel over naval rights of way. With specialized features such as solid bones, small wings, and posterior legs, loons are highly adapted to their aquatic lifestyle. Spending time observing even an overwintering loon, nature lovers can experience an intangible wilderness spirit in place, time, and circumstance.

Western Grebe

(Aechmophorus occidentalis)

Western Grebes breed entirely inland, cheating coastal residents out of the opportunity to enjoy one of nature's greatest courtship shows. Although most west coast residents have never seen the grebe's spectacular dashes across the surface of a prairie slough, they are fortunate to have unsurpassed concentrations of this winter visitor.

The distinguished look of the Western Grebe is refined by its formal plumage, ruby eyes, cobra-like head, and long stiletto bill. It is easily identified by its long, graceful neck, as it fishes the open waters of bays, harbours, and lagoons, piercing deep-bodied fish with its dagger-like bill.

Horned Grebe

(*Podiceps auritus*)

Like many waterbirds that winter on the coast, Horned Grebes lose the splendour of their summer plumage and assume low-key black and white colouring. Horned Grebes are abundant in shallow, protected bays from September through March; they exhibit peppy behaviour as they leap up before diving neatly headfirst.

All grebes have the seemingly strange habit of eating feathers, occasionally packing their digestive tracts. One explanation for this is that grebes use feathers to dislodge the bones and scales of their fishy prey from their digestive systems. Grebes also have very unusual feet. Unlike the fully webbed feet of ducks, gulls, cormorants, and alcids, the toes of grebes are individually lobed, not webbed.

Pied-billed Grebe
(*Podilymbus podiceps*)

The small, squat, drab body of the Pied-billed Grebe seems perfectly suited to its marshy habitat, but its loud whooping is strangely foreign. The distinctive *kuk-kuk-cow-cow-cow-cowp-cowp* is a sound that seems more at home in tropical rainforests than murky cattail wetlands.

Pied-billed Grebes can be found—or at least heard—on most freshwater wetlands that are surrounded by emergent vegetation such as cattails and bullrushes. These small grebes are frustrating to follow as they appear and disappear effortlessly from the reedy margins of the marsh. Only in the worst winter weather do Pied-billed Grebes retreat from their cozy wetlands, to wait out the freeze-up uncomfortably in the waves and weeds of the ocean.

American Coot
(*Fulica americana*)

The highly versatile American Coot is a delightful mix of confusion and comedy—it has the lobed toes of a grebe, the bill of a chicken, and the black body and swimming habits of a duck. However, the American Coot is not remotely related to any of these species; its closest coastal cousins are the rails and cranes. American Coots dabble, dive, walk on land, eat plant or animal matter and can be found in ponds, lakes, marshes, salt bays, lagoons or city parks.

These loud, grouchy birds are seen chugging along in wetlands, their heads bobbing in time with their paddling feet. At peak speed, this back and forth motion escalates and seems to disorient the American Coot. It will fake a take-off by running and flapping to the other side of the wetland.

Double-crested Cormorant

(*Phalacrocorax auritus*)

The Double-crested Cormorant is the only cormorant that ventures inland, and it is a common sight on the west coast. Somewhere in the evolutionary process, cormorants lost (or perhaps had never acquired) the ability to waterproof their wings, so they need to dry their wings after each swim. These large black waterbirds are often seen perched on sea walls, bridge pilings, and buoys, with their wings partially spread, exposing their wet feathers to sun and wind.

It would seem to be a great disadvantage for a waterbird to have to dry its wings, but the cormorant's ability to wet its feathers decreases its buoyancy, making it easier for it to swim after the fish on which it preys. Sealed nostrils, a long rudder-like tail, and excellent underwater vision also complement the Double-crested Cormorants' aquatic lifestyle.

Pelagic Cormorant
(Phalacrocorax pelagicus)

This prehistoric-looking bird is the smallest and slimmest cormorant of the west coast and is commonly seen flying, single-file, low over open water. Unlike the Double-crested Cormorant, which holds a kink in its neck when it flies, the Pelagic Cormorant flies with its neck outstretched. During spring and summer, this sleek, glossy sea bird sports two distinctive white patches on its rump.

Cormorants are one of the few birds that are best appreciated from a distance. Our overly sensitive sense of smell and biased perception of beauty don't promote many return trips to cormorant colonies. Pelagic Cormorants nest precariously on thin cliff ledges, laying their eggs into a meagre nest of seaweed and guano.

Trumpeter Swan

(Cygnus buccinator)

Once valued for its great feathers, soft skin, and tasty meat, the magnificent Trumpeter Swan is slowly regaining the range it lost early this century. The west coast swan populations of the 1930s were the last hope for our largest waterfowl, one of the first birds to be protected by law. With a safer environment, the Trumpeter Swan population is growing and expanding into territory it occupied in the past. These swans, named for their loud, resonant call, overwinter along the coast, frequenting sheltered bays, estuaries, and farmers' fields.

The Trumpeter Swan's relative, the Tundra Swan, is smaller, with a yellow teardrop on its bill. It migrates through in smaller numbers.

Mute Swan
(*Cygnus olor*)

As its name suggests, the Mute Swan is a relatively quiet bird, resorting to loud hissing only when seriously threatened. Its unequalled grace led some people to introduce it to North America from Eurasia, and feral populations have been established in a few isolated areas.

Unlike all other large white birds on the west coast, swans do not have black wing tips. The only contrasts with their all-white plumage are their feet, eyes, and bill. Although the artistic pose the Mute Swan casts is splendid, beneath the silky white plumage is a powerful bird—one that can viciously peck an unwary wanderer, leaving welts and wounds on any area of the body within striking distance.

Snow Goose

(Anser caerulescens)

    Anyone who has witnessed tens of thousands of Snow Geese lifting in unison will not soon forget the experience—black-tipped wings contrast with clean white plumage in a cloud of life. Instead of flying in well-formed 'Vs,' Snow Geese fly in loose, wavy lines, yelping noisily. The large white birds fuel up in estuaries and marshes, then continue their northern migration to their Arctic breeding grounds. Many of the Snow Geese seen moving along the coast will not nest until they reach their breeding grounds on Russia's Wrangle Island.

    Coastal residents are fortunate indeed: these thrills are not restricted to the migration—thousands of Snow Geese overwinter along the large river deltas.

Canada Goose
(*Branta canadensis*)

Most flocks of Canada Geese encountered in city parks and golf courses are residents that show little concern for their human neighbours. These urban geese seem to think nothing of creating a traffic jam or blocking a fairway, while dining on lawns and gardens.

Migrating Canada Geese also visit the coast. These geese look just like their urban counterparts, but behave much differently. If the spoiled urban geese become tiresome, find an estuary, and watch as a honking flock of geese lifts and forms its distinctive 'V.'

Breeding pairs are legendarily loyal. They mate for life, and not only will a widowed goose often remain unpaired for the rest of its life, it's also common for a mate to stay at the side of a fallen partner.

Brant

(Branta bernicla)

   The local eelgrass beds spread out along the west coast are like welcome truck stops for this small marine goose. Thousands of migrating Brant move north in spring and south in autumn, flying from one good eelgrass spot to another. The exposed bars and sandflats on which they feed and preen can be packed with the black geese during spring migration.

   Brant are truly geese of the salt water. They are seen inland infrequently, even during their migration from the Pacific Coast to the Arctic Ocean. Though smaller than and lacking the white cheek of Canada Geese, Brant are also sociable, and form long-term pair bonds.

Mallard

(Anas platyrhychos)

The Mallard is the classic duck of inland marshes—the male's iridescent green head and chestnut breast are symbolic of wetland habitat. This large duck is commonly seen feeding year-round in city parks, small lakes, and farmers' fields. With their legs positioned under the middle part of their bodies, Mallards walk easily, and they can spring straight out of water without a running start.

Male Mallards pursue females energetically, but a male will soon abandon his mate after she's laid her eggs. This lack of parental commitment may seem harsh, but in fact it benefits the female and the ducklings. A colourful father would likely attract the attention of predators, placing the lives of the well-camouflaged female and ducklings at risk.

American Wigeon

(Anas americana)

The male American Wigeon looks and sounds somewhat like an old-timer—the white forehead and grey sides of this medium-sized duck's head look like a balding scalp and the slow, nasal *wee-he-he-he-he* call sounds like a wheezy laugh. Broad green patches extend back from the male's eyes, almost as if his laughing had brought tears to his eyes and caused his green mascara to run.

Like the other dabbling ducks of the coast, the American Wigeon lays about 10 eggs in a well-concealed nest; hatching begins in about 25 days. The ducklings leave the nest almost immediately and grow quickly; in 50 days the first of the young begin to fly. From mid-October through April, resident populations are supplemented by thousands of over-wintering American Wigeons from the interior and the prairies.

Lesser Scaup

(Aythya affinis)

The Lesser Scaup is the Oreo cookie of the coastal ducks— black at both ends and white in the middle. During mild winters, the Lesser Scaup is common on lakes, harbours, estuaries, and lagoons.

The Lesser Scaup is a diving duck; unlike dabbling ducks, diving ducks have their legs placed well back on their bodies. This is advantageous for underwater swimming, but it makes walking difficult. All ducks are front-heavy, so in order for diving ducks to stand, they must raise their front ends high to maintain balance. As a result, Lesser Scaup are clumsy on land, but they regain their dignity when they take to water.

Surf Scoter
(*Melanitta perspicillata*)

Tough, big, and stocky, scoters prefer strength to grace. Scoters are deep-diving sea ducks; stormy weather amounts to nothing more than a simple annoyance in their feeding habits. Surf Scoters are frequently observed among white-capped waves; they dive to wrench shellfish from rocks with their sturdy bills and swallow the shellfish whole.

Surf Scoters form rafts (large concentrations of floating ducks) on the Pacific Coast during winter months. In spring, these large black ducks migrate inland to northern lakes and tundra ponds. On the choppy sea or a large boreal lake, Surf Scoters live up to their name by 'scooting' across the water's surface, occasionally crashing through incoming waves.

Harlequin Duck

(Histrionicus histrionicus)

Bobbing like colourful corks, Harlequin Ducks seem almost unsinkable—in spite of their preference for turbulent and chaotic habitats. During winter, the small, round ducks can be seen precariously close to breaking surf, but 'Harlies' seem unconcerned by their dangerous environment.

During summer, Harlequin Ducks leave the coast and go inland to seek out the most turbulent mountain streams. In these frothing waters, the drably coloured female is left to raise the brood of ducklings. This lack of romance and commitment may seem to contradict this duck's unusual name, however 'Harlequin' refers to a colourfully made-up actor, not a melodramatic romance novel.

Common Goldeneye

(Bucephala clangula)

The entertaining courtship display of this widespread duck is one of nature's best slapstick routines. The spry male goldeneye rapidly arches its large green head backward until his bill points skyward, producing a seemingly painful *Kraaaagh*. Completely unaffected by his chiropractic wonder, he continuously performs this ritual to mainly disinterested hens. Feeding off the female's apathy, the male escalates his performance, creating a comedic spring scene that is appreciated more by birdwatchers than by the intended audience. When the female finally relents and pays attention to the quality of the various displays, the eager male, seemingly aware of his tenuous situation, reacts quickly, finalizing the pair's bond on the water's surface.

Barrow's Goldeneye

(Bucephala islandica)

Only days old, small goldeneye chicks are lured out of the only world they know by their pleading mother. Although this seems typical of most ducks, young Barrow's Goldeneye require more coaxing than most—their nest is an old woodpecker hole high in a tree. With a faith-filled leap, the cottonball-soft ducklings tumble towards the ground, often bouncing on impact before following their mother through the dense underbrush to the nearest water.

Much of the world's population of Barrow's Goldeneye begins life by tumbling out of trees in B.C., Oregon, and Washington. Although female goldeneye closely resemble one another, a male Barrow's Goldeneye can be distinguished from its Common counterpart by the white crescent on its face and the white 'fingerprints' on its back.

Bufflehead

(Bucephala albeola)

Held in the highest regard by naturalists, the small fluffy Bufflehead is the 'cutest' duck in North America. A very reserved duck, the Bufflehead has simple plumage and a rotund physique. Found during winter on just about every inland lake, pond, and wetland, Buffleheads are rarely seen discrediting themselves by accepting handouts from humans.

Like their close relative the goldeneye, Buffleheads nest in cavities and have quite large heads. They were named for the shape of their head, which reminded an early ornithologist of a buffalo's. Regardless of head shape, the white slice behind the male's eye is distinctive, because it does not have an outline.

Hooded Merganser

(Lophodytes cucullatus)

Lacking diverse facial expressions, many non-human animals have evolved other means of sharing their feelings with others of their species. When aroused by danger or passion, a male Hooded Merganser flares his distinctive white crest. Unfortunately for the 'Hoodies,' many persistent birders are not satisfied until the crest is raised in alarm, producing a re-markable pose. The intrusion often causes the male to retreat, foregoing his everyday business at the expense of an overzealous birder. These mini-mergansers are delightful, and can be appreciated at a distance at many wooded lakes, all along the west coast.

Common Merganser
(Mergus merganser)

Looking like a large jumbo jet taking off, the Common Merganser runs along the surface of the water, beating its heavy wings, until sufficient speed is reached for lift-off. Once in the air, our largest duck looks compressed and arrow-like as it flies strongly in low, straight lines.

Mergansers are lean and powerful waterfowl, designed for the underwater pursuit of fish. Unlike the bills of other fishers, a merganser's bill is saw-like, serrated to ensure that its squirmy, slimy prey does not escape. Common Mergansers are cavity nesters, breeding wherever there are suitable lakes and trees, and they are often seen on rivers. On the coast, resident populations of this majestic duck are boosted by the arrival of inland breeders during the winter months.

Tufted Puffin
(*Fratercula cirrhata*)

The extravagant look of the Tufted Puffin is short-lived, for like antlers on deer the remarkable plates on the puffin's beak are shed after they've served the purpose of attracting a female and reinforcing the pair bond. The elegant blond plumes streaming back from the bird's eyes are also lost late in summer, as the puffin prepares for its eight-month retreat on the open sea.

The Tufted Puffin is one of the most popular birds with west coast birdwatchers. Since it breeds on only a few remote rocky islands that have grassy burrowing sites, it is seen infrequently by all but the most committed or extremely fortunate birdwatcher. Tufted Puffins aren't likely to become more common—a significant number of this special sea bird drowns each year, entangled in gill nets.

Pigeon Guillemot
(Cepphus columba)

Pigeon Guillemots are common sea birds, foraging near shore and nesting on rocky cliff ledges. Guillemots race through air and water like a needle pulling stitches through cloth—a confusing chase for a pursuing rival. The solid black plumage surrounding a white wing patch is offset by the guillemot's radiant red mouth-lining and feet. These scarlet accents are flaunted outrageously during their courtship rituals, when guillemots wave their feet and then peer down the throat of their potential mates. These bold markings enable birders to easily spot Pigeon Guillemots nesting on slate-grey cliffs.

Marbled Murrelet
(*Brachyramphus marmoratus*)

This endangered sea bird outsmarted the greatest North American ornithologists for several centuries, and scientists were unable to find a single nest until 1974. As with many brain teasers, the answer to this great birding mystery was not uncovered by an academic with an endless list of degrees; it was solved by an attentive amateur. Unlikely as it seems, this stubby sea bird, far more adapted to life in the open water, nests 200 feet up, on mossy tree limbs. Its grouse-like breeding plumage should have been a major clue in the mystery, but hindsight is not what this bird currently needs. Dependent on coastal old growth forests, the Marbled Murrelet is declining as a direct result of logging practices, an almost inconceivable notion for a bird that spends ten months of the year drifting at sea.

Common Murre

(Uria aagle)

Like all true alcids, Common Murres fly nervously. Their tiny wings, designed for pursuing fish underwater, beat the air feverishly, attempting to maintain speed. Like uncontrolled missiles, murres veer from side to side as they rocket toward a steep, rocky cliff. On the thin, ledged nest site, Common Murres lay their pear-shaped eggs on bare rock. The egg is designed to roll in a tight circle; the precarious nest site offers no room for error.

Many birds that overwinter on the surface of the open ocean share the countershading colouration of the murre. From above, the dark back blends with the steely sea, while submerged predators cannot find the light-coloured underbelly against the bright sky. The number of Common Murres appears to swell during the winter, as these birds disperse from their concentrated breeding colonies into inlets, bays, and channels.

Common Tern
(*Sterna hirundo*)

The Common Tern generally goes unnoticed until a splash draws attention to its head-first dives into water. Once it has firmly seized a small fish in its black-tipped bill, the tern bounces back into the air and continues its leisurely flight.

Although terns and gulls share many of the same physical characteristics, there are features which clearly separate the two groups. Terns seldom rest on the water, and they rarely soar in flight. They also have very short necks, pointed wings and long, forked tails, and they tend to look towards the ground during flight. These characteristics, along with the fact that its black cap does not extend below its eye, should help identify the Common Tern.

Bonaparte's Gull
(*Larus philadelphia*)

This delicate, black-headed gull has few of its family's disturbing habits. Bonaparte's Gulls are not usually seen in cities and parks—their scratchy little calls are frequently heard close to the sea, where they can be seen feeding communally on the water's surface. Most Bonaparte's Gulls leave the coast for the summer to breed in the boreal forest, where they nest, in most un-gull-like fashion, high in spruce trees.

Outside the summer breeding season, most Bonaparte's Gulls lose their distinctive black hoods, but retain flashy white wing patches and a noticeable black spot behind their eyes. This gull was named not after the famed French emperor, but after his nephew, Charles Lucien Bonaparte, who brought recognition to his family's name through the relatively non-violent world of ornithology.

Glaucous-winged Gull

(Larus glaucescens)

Many gulls come and go on the west coast, but the Glaucous-winged Gull is a year-round resident. Large flocks of this gull can be found in bays, estuaries, freshwater lakes, garbage dumps, city parks, and agricultural fields. Glaucous-winged Gulls are dispersed so widely they are sure to be sighted on just about any birding trip taken along the Canadian side of the Pacific Coast. A very similar species, the Western Gull, becomes more common as you enter the U.S., and many hybrids of the two species live near the border.

Despite their abundance on the west coast, the Glaucous-winged Gull is rare inland, and its appearance can cause quite a stir in a community of landlocked birders.

Great Blue Heron

(Ardea herodias)

The Great Blue Heron is one of the largest coastal birds. It often stands motionless as it surveys the calm waters, its graceful lines blending naturally with the dancing grasses and cattails of inland wetlands, or the waves breaking on the coast.

This great sentry is familiar to most west coast residents, as its large size and regal appearance are difficult to overlook. Great Blue Herons are often seen in surprisingly large numbers, evenly spaced in favourite hunting spots. A metaphor of patience, a hunting heron will not strike out with its cocked bill until it can be assured of a meal. In flight, Great Blue Herons are just as laid back, their lazy wingbeats slowly but effortlessly carrying them to their tree-top nests.

Black Oystercatcher

(Haematopus bachmani)

For animals that prey exclusively on shellfish the trick is not catching clams, oysters, mussels, and barnacles. Shellfish are abundant in west coast tidal pools, and just about any animal capable of movement can chase down an oyster. The Black Oystercatcher's remarkable bill allows this specialized bird to insert its bill within partially opened bivalves and slice the hinge muscle. Because of this shucking structure, and their ability to jackhammer shells, oystercatchers are able to exploit a food source unavailable to most other birds.

On islets and rocky shores, Black Oystercatchers are often seen in small groups. This year-round resident's frantic high-pitched call, button-like yellow eyes, bright red bill, and sturdy legs contribute to its unmistakable character.

Lesser Yellowlegs
(*Tringa flavipes*)

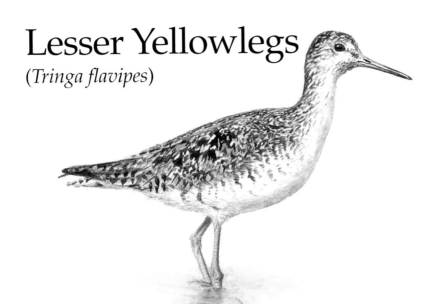

All shorebirds are difficult to identify, but to beginning birders the sandpipers that lack bold characteristics are a particular cause of frustration. To those birders, the relatively long, yellow legs are characteristic of a yellowlegs.

As birders gain more experience, they enjoy the challenge of separating the Greater and the Lesser Yellowlegs. The Lesser has a relatively thin, all-black bill. The Greater, which is more common on the west coast (but don't let that bias your identification), has a slightly up-turned bill—so slightly that you see it one moment and not the next. Generally, the Lesser calls with two *tews*, and the Greater calls with three. Experienced birders will name them at a glance, but even more experienced birders will tell you that many of these people are bluffing, and that much of the time you can only write 'unidentified Yellowlegs' in your field notes.

Killdeer

(Charadrius vociferus)

The Killdeer is probably the most wide-spread shorebird on the coast. It nests on gravelly shorelines, utility rights-of-way, lawns, pastures, and occasionally on gravel roofs within cities. Its name is a paraphrase of its distinctive loud call, *kill-dee kill-dee kill-deer*, and isn't an indication of its hunting habits.

The Killdeer's response to predators relies on deception and good acting skills. To divert a predator's attention away from a nest or a brood of young, an adult Killdeer will flop around to feign an injury (usually a broken wing or leg). Once the Killdeer has the attention of the fox, crow, or gull, it leads the predator away from the vulnerable nest. After it reaches a safe distance, the adult Killdeer is suddenly 'healed' and flies off, leaving the predator without a meal.

Dunlin

(*Calidris alpina*)

These small, plump shorebirds are not in and of themselves remarkable—Dunlin are communal creatures, and it is the spectacular clouds of Dunlin that hold the magic of this species: individuals flying wingtip to wingtip, instantaneously changing course, tens of thousands behaving as one. These hypnotic flights, flashing alternating shades of white and black, are commonly seen as Dunlin overwinter on west coast estuaries and bays.

It's humbling to know that, despite our human intelligence, we cannot perform feats routine to a tiny-brained Dunlin. The unexplained communal flight of Dunlin leads many thoughtful observers to question accepted theories on social communication—profound questions drawn from the habits of a simple bird.

Black-bellied Plover

(*Pluvialis squatarola*)

During the winter months, Black-bellied Plovers are commonly seen darting along open shorelines, grassy openings, and ploughed fields. The robin-like run-stop foraging technique is very distinctive of this long-legged bird. Although they are dressed in greys for much of their west coast winter retreat, during early spring and late autumn many Black-bellied Plovers continue to wear their summer tuxedo plumage.

Although not all walks along the beach will bring an encounter with shorebirds, a keen birdwatcher will be able to determine which has been there before, because sandpipers have four toes whereas the three-toed tracks of plovers lack a hind digit.

Spotted Sandpiper

(*Actitis macularia*)

This common shorebird of the coast, lakes, and rivers has a most uncommon mating strategy. In a reversal of the gender roles of most birds, female Spotted Sandpipers compete for males in the spring. After the nest is built and the eggs are laid, the female leaves to find another mate, while the male incubates the eggs. This behaviour is repeated up to five times before the female settles down with the last male to raise the chicks.

Spotted Sandpipers are readily identified by their arthritic-looking, stiff-winged flight, low over the water. Although Spotted Sandpipers lose the distinctive patterning on their breast for much of the year, their habit of bobbing their tails up and down continues year-round.

Bald Eagle
(Haliaeetus leucocephalus)

Bald Eagle heaven must look very much like the Pacific Coast. Salmon runs, concentrated waterfowl, washed-up carcasses, and Osprey to pirate food from ensure that west coast Bald Eagles rarely go hungry. Easy-living eagles spend much of their lives perched high in trees overlooking bays, watching the dynamics of nature unfold.

Bald Eagles are adept at catching fish, which they pluck just below the water's surface, but the national emblem of the United States is equally satisfied with a meal requiring less effort. A Bald Eagle takes four or five years to acquire its distinctive white tail and head, but the younger birds are easily distinguished by their two-metre (6 1/2-foot) wingspan.

Osprey
(Pandion haliaetus)

On bent wings, an Osprey surveys the calm water of a coastal bay. Spotting a flash of silver at the water's surface, the Osprey folds in its great wings and dives towards the fish. An instant before striking the water, the large raptor thrusts its talons forward to grasp its slippery prey. The Osprey may completely disappear beneath the water to ensure a successful hunt, then it reappears, slapping its wings on the surface as it regains flight. Once it has regained the air, holding its prey facing forward, the Osprey shakes off the residual water and heads off towards its bulky stick nest.

A hungry Bald Eagle witnessing this remarkable hunting feat will not hesitate to pirate the meal. For many Osprey, a duel with a larger eagle is not worth the prized fish, so the fish is dropped and the Osprey returns to scan the steely surface of the sea.

Red-tailed Hawk

(*Buteo jamaicensis*)

With its fierce facial expression and untidy feathers, the Red-tailed Hawk looks like it has been suddenly and rudely awakened. You would think other coastal birds would treat this large raptor with more respect, but the Red-tailed Hawk is constantly being chased by crows, jays, and blackbirds.

The Red-tailed Hawk is well named, but it isn't until this hawk is two or three years old that its tail becomes brick red. The black 'belt' around its midsection and a dark leading edge to its wings are better field marks because they're seen in most red tails. Look for these common hawks soaring above open country with nearby woodlands.

Northern Harrier

(Circus cyaneus)

This common marsh hawk can best be identified by its behaviour. No other coastal raptor is often seen flying low over fields and pastures. The slow, lazy wingbeats of the Northern Harrier coincide with its undulating, erratic flight pattern. Unlike other hawks, which can find their prey only visually, the Northern Harrier stays close enough to the ground to listen for the birds, voles, and mice on which it feeds.

All harriers have a distinctive white rump. Females and young Northern Harriers are predominantly brown, and males are dressed in grey. These long-tailed and long-winged hawks nest on the ground in long grasses, shrubs, and wet meadows.

Cooper's Hawk
(*Accipiter cooperi*)

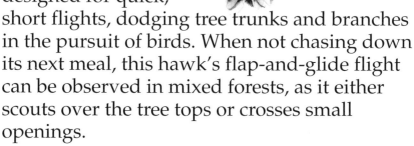

This medium-sized forest hawk is infrequently seen because it does not habitually ride rising thermals. The Cooper's Hawk is designed for quick, short flights, dodging tree trunks and branches in the pursuit of birds. When not chasing down its next meal, this hawk's flap-and-glide flight can be observed in mixed forests, as it either scouts over the tree tops or crosses small openings.

The hawk's short, rounded wings, long, rudder-like tail, and long, piercing talons enable this raptor to prey almost exclusively on birds, which it frequently seizes in mid-air. Cooper's Hawks sometimes visit backyard feeders—not for the millet and sunflower seeds, but for the sparrows and finches the food attracts.

Peregrine Falcon

(Falco peregrinus)

The Peregrine Falcon is the fastest animal in the world: it can reach speeds of up to 290 km/hr (170 mph). Even the fastest ducks and shorebirds have little chance of escaping this effective predator. The Peregrine Falcon plunges on its prey, punches it in mid-air and follows it to the ground, where it kills and eats its victim.

Peregrine Falcons are among the birds most seriously affected by the use of agricultural pesticides such as DDT; the pesticides accumulate in their bodies and reduce their breeding efficiency. The west coast Peregrines have not been affected to the same degree as inland birds because they have an abundant year-round food supply, and do not need to migrate. Along the rocky shorelines of the west coast, they remain common, delighting and astonishing wildlife viewers with their extraordinary hunting skills.

Great Horned Owl
(Bubo virginianus)

This common nocturnal hunter is among the most formidable of coastal predators. Great Horned Owls use both their specialized hearing and their human-sized eyes to hunt mice, rabbits, quail, amphibians, and occasionally, fish. They have a poorly developed sense of smell, which may be why these owls are the only consistent predator of skunks. Worn-out and discarded Great Horned Owl feathers are therefore often identifiable by a simple sniff.

The deep, resonant hooting of the Great Horned Owl is easily imitated, often leading to enjoyable exchanges between bird and birder. The coastal Great Horned Owl is the largest owl in North America, its distinctive silhouette a frequent sight on moonlit nights.

Spotted Owl
(Strix occidentalis)

Tucked against a great trunk, perched on a mossy limb, the Spotted Owl begins its nightly hunt. The soft brown eyes and deadly accurate ears scan the darkening forest for motion. A rustle, a twitch—a vole scurries a distance away. Excited, the owl orients itself to the noise by systematically jerking its head—up, down, and side to side—cueing itself to the rodent's sound. On silent wings, the Spotted Owl launches itself and floats down to the darkened forest floor. Crashing through ferns and shrubs, the owl seizes the vole, crushing it with its strong, sharp talons. After swallowing the rodent whole, the owl flies lazily back up to its perch, patiently awaiting the next vole to unknowingly challenge the owl's hunting instincts.

This hunting scene, played out for so many generations, is becoming rare as the old growth forests this owl needs for survival disappear.

Western Screech-Owl

(Otus kennicotti)

Despite its small size, the Western Screech-Owl is a mighty hunter, with a varied diet ranging from insects it catches in mid-air to grouse that outweigh this small owl. Silent and reclusive by day, Screech Owls leave their daytime roosts to hunt at night.

Owls' senses are refined for darkness and silence. Their forward-facing eyes have many times more light-gathering sensors than ours do, and their wings are edged with frayed feathers for silent flight. Their ears, located on the sides of their heads, are asymmetrical (one is higher than the other), giving these birds stereoscopic hearing that enables them to track sounds more easily. Given all these adaptations, it is to no one's surprise that owls have successfully invaded nearly all of the world's ecosystems.

Turkey Vulture
(*Cathartes aura*)

The Turkey Vulture's seemingly effortless soaring is made possible by its great, silver-lined wings. Turkey Vultures seldom flap their wings, and they often rock from side to side as they scan forest clearings and coastlines. The way their wings angle upwards in a shallow 'V' is a useful clue to their identification.

Turkey Vultures depend completely on carrion (dead animals) for food, and they have evolved a keen sense of smell. Their heads are featherless to keep them clean and parasite-free while they dig around inside carcasses. The Turkey Vulture's habit of regurgitating its rotting meal may be a defence mechanism that allows adults to reduce their weight for a quicker take-off, and gives the young vultures a powerful deterrent to would-be predators, who would prefer their food to smell a little fresher.

Ruffed Grouse

(*Bonasa umbellus*)

Hikers are often amazed at the Ruffed Grouse. It is not this bird's voice, plumage, or spectacular flights that draw attention to it—rather it's the Ruffed Grouse's habit of doing nothing. For this poorly understood behaviour, the terms used to describe Ruffed Grouse are often very unflattering.

It is not out of stupidity that Ruffed Grouse freeze, remaining motionless despite the advances of curious onlookers. In reality, this adaptation serves this and other grouse well, because their plumage provides the birds with effective camouflage. It's probable that for every Ruffed Grouse that is encountered, many more are overlooked, thanks to their defence behaviour. It is likely, therefore, that in the majority of Ruffed Grouse-human interactions, it is the birds who marvel smugly at the dull-sensed passersby.

Blue Grouse

(Dendragapus obscurus)

In the densely forested mountains and hills that rise up from the Pacific Coast, the Blue Grouse performs its annual courtship song. The love call the male emits is deep, so low that the human ear can hear only a fraction of the sounds. From around the forest, the owl-like hooting attracts an audience of hens to an elaborate courtship dance.

The female's approval is displayed by another series of deep call notes. This auditory reinforcement is so stimulating to the male that Blue Grouse males have been known to intimately investigate tape machines playing the female's response. These large woodland grouse are a western specialty, their interesting behaviours easily discovered by coastal naturalists.

California Quail

(Callipepla californica)

    With their distinctive forward-facing plume, California Quails look similar to dancers who performed in North America during the 1920s. With head gear similar to that of flappers, California Quail scutter quickly around their stages in tight, cohesive groups.

    At the northern extreme of their range, the California Quail is an exotic bird, introduced from southern sources. Following the range of this small quail south, it is unclear where the natural limit once was. Regardless of the confusion about the California Quail's natural history, it is appreciated throughout its current range, and is the state bird of California. The endearing contact call it makes when separated from its covey is a distinctive and appropriate *where are you?*

Common Raven

(*Corvus corax*)

The largest and most intelligent of the songbirds has a dignified presence about it. Whether stealing food from under the snout of a grizzly, harassing a Bald Eagle in mid-air, or confidently strutting among campers at a favourite park, the Raven is worthy of its reputation as a clever bird. Glorified in traditional cultures worldwide, including those of coastal aboriginals, Ravens are not restricted to the instinctive behaviours of most other birds. With the ability to express themselves playfully, tumbling aimlessly through the air or sliding down a snowy bank on their backs, these large, raucous birds flaunt traits many think of as being exclusively human. By behaving unexpectedly, Common Ravens teach us their greatest lessons, reminding us how little insight we have into the non-human world.

Northwestern Crow

(Corvus caurinus)

    The Northwestern Crow, so commonly encountered in farmyards and city parks and along forest edges and shorelines, is very limited in its overall range. Though extremely similar to the American Crow, which is widespread inland, the Northwestern Crow ranges only along the Pacific Coast north of Oregon. Whether this bird is a distinct species from its relative is a concern most novice birdwatchers postpone to a future time.

    There is no doubt that this coastal bird is a crow. Its loud habits and adaptability are characteristics that don't go unnoticed by human observers. Northwestern Crows show a wide range of food preferences, including one for shellfish, which they drop from the air onto rocks, cracking the shells to expose the meaty flesh.

Red-winged Blackbird
(*Agelaius phoeniceus*)

No cattail marsh is free from the loud calls and bossy, aggressive nature of the Red-winged Blackbird. The male's bright red shoulders are his most important tool in the often strategic and intricate displays he uses to defend his territory from rivals. In experiments, males whose red shoulders were painted black soon lost their territories to rivals that they had previously defeated.

The female's interest lies not in the individual combatants, but in nesting habitat, and a male who can successfully defend a large area of dense cattails will breed with many females. After the females have built their concealed nests and laid their eggs, the male must continue his constant vigil against intruders and predators.

Brown-headed Cowbird

(Molothrus ater)

This small black bird with a chocolate-brown head is quickly becoming one of the most hated native birds in North America. Their treatment of other songbirds frustrates many bird enthusiasts.

Historically, Brown-headed Cowbirds followed the bison, so these vagabonds were constantly on the move and were unable to tend a nest. To overcome this problem, cowbirds laid their eggs in the nests of other songbirds, which raised the young cowbirds as their own. Unfortunately for the unwilling host, the young cowbirds are very aggressive, and will win out over the foster parent's own offspring, who often die from lack of food. Cowbirds now follow ranch mammals, and the ultimate blame for the parasitism of over 140 bird species lies with the expansion of ranching and the fragmentation of forests, which have significantly increased the cowbird's range.

European Starling
(*Sturnus vulgaris*)

In 1890, 60 European Starlings were introduced in New York's Central Park, as part of the New York Shakespearean Society's plan to introduce to their city all the birds mentioned in their favourite author's plays. Starlings are continually expanding their range at the expense of native birds, colonizing many islands off-shore.

These highly adaptable birds, which are often confused with blackbirds, have short tails, and a bright yellow bill to complement their iridescent breeding plumage. Starlings are accomplished mimics, and can confuse birdwatchers by imitating the calls of many of the species with which they are associated.

Steller's Jay
(*Cyanocitta stelleri*)

While most North Americans are treated to the extroverted and often mischievous behaviour of the Blue Jay, west coast residents experience those traits in the Steller's Jay. The beauty of the provincial bird of British Columbia is too often overlooked, overshadowed as it is by this jay's bold and boisterous personality. Often drifting into coastal cities in late autumn and winter, they noisily announce their arrival with their unavoidable call, *shack-shack-shack*. A permanent and historic resident west of the Rocky Mountains, the Steller's Jay should be viewed as a unique character of the west coast. This proud bird is unknown to most North Americans, and eastern birdwatchers often envy their western counterparts for having the chance to sight them.

American Robin

(Turdus migratorius)

The robin is much more than a common backyard bird with a flute-like voice. The robin's close relationship with urban areas has allowed many coastal residents an insight into a bird's social and ecological role. A robin dashing around a yard in search of worms or ripe berries is as familiar to many people as its three-part song, *cheerily-cheery up-cheerio*. Robins make up part of the emotional landscape of coastal communities, as their song, their young's hatching and fast development, and occasionally even their deaths, are experiences shared by their human neighbours.

Varied Thrush

(Ixoreus naevius)

The haunting courtship song of the Varied Thrush is unlike any other sound in nature. Western residents alone are blessed by the long steam-whistle notes, delivered at well-spaced alternating pitches, opening and closing cool, damp spring days.

This counterpart of the robin is most often found deep in the mature rainforest running along the west coast. Varied Thrushes are secretive, and their simple song and dress grant these birds a nobility that few others possess. When nature's banquet is sparse or winter storms blanket the coastal ranges with heavy snows, Varied Thrushes often retreat from their coniferous temples to urban areas, where they feed in backyard feeders and on ornamental shrubs. However, when the coolest winter days have passed, most Varied Thrushes regain their dignified place in the moist woodlands, proclaiming spring with a song that cuts through the heavy air.

Swainson's Thrush

(Catharus ustulatus)

Beauty in forest birds is often gauged by sound and not sight. Given this criterion, the Swainson's Thrush is certainly one of the most beautiful birds to inhabit coastal woodlands. A migrant to the coastal rainforests, the Swainson's Thrush are rarely seen during their all too brief five-month stay, revealing themselves only when flocking together for the southern migration.

The upward spiral in the song of the Swainson's Thrush lifts the soul with each note, and leaves a fortunate listener breathless at its conclusion. The inspiring song is heard in early spring mornings, but is most appreciated at dusk, when the Swainson's Thrush alone offers a melody to the dark, empty forest.

Rock Dove

(Columba livia)

The Rock Dove (or Pigeon) is very dependent on human society for food and shelter. This European native lives in old buildings and on ledges and bridges, and it feeds primarily on waste grain and human handouts. Although these common city birds appear strained when walking—their heads moving back and forth with every step—few birds are as swift in flight.

Rock Doves are perfectly woven into rural and urban life on the coast, and they are abundant in city parks. While no other coastal bird varies as much in colouration, a white, red, blue, or mixed Pigeon will always have a flashy white rump.

Belted Kingfisher
(*Ceryle alcyon*)

This medium-sized bird is always associated with water. As its name suggests, kingfishers prey primarily on fish, which they catch with precise headfirst dives. A dead branch extending over calm water will often serve as a suitable perch for the Belted Kingfisher to survey the fish below.

These year-round residents can be found near open water, but are never far from shore. They build their nests at the ends of burrows, often dug a metre (1.09 yards) deep into a sandy bank. A rattling call, blue-grey colouration, and large crest are the distinctive features of the Belted Kingfisher. With most coastal birds, the males are more colourful, but female Kingfishers are distinguished from males by the presence of a second rust-coloured belt.

Common Nighthawk
(Chordeiles minor)

This common coastal bird, which is unrelated to true hawks, has two distinct personalities—mild-mannered by day, it rests on the ground or on a horizontal tree branch, its colour and shape blending perfectly into the texture of the bark. At dusk, the Common Nighthawk takes on a new form as a dazzling and erratic flyer, catching insects in flight.

To many people, the call of the nighthawk is a sound of summer evenings. The fascinating courtship of Common Nighthawks occurs over forest openings, beaches, and occasionally, urban areas. The nighthawks repeatedly call out with a loud, nasal *peeent* as they circle high overhead, then they dive suddenly towards the ground and create a hollow 'vroom' sound by thrusting their wings forward at the last possible moment, pulling out of the dive.

Rufous-sided Towhee

(Pipilo erythrophthalmus)

    This large, cocky sparrow is most often heard in the dense understorey before it is seen. The Rufous-sided Towhee's characteristic double-scratching foraging technique rustles the dead leaves and grass beneath dense thickets. 'Squeaking' (kissing the back of your hand) or 'pishing' (puckering up and saying *pish* as loudly and as wetly as possible) is irresistible for towhees, who will quickly pop out from the cover and investigate the curious noise.

    The male's black hood, white chest, and red flanks are characteristic of his species alone. With binoculars in bright light, you can also see this bird's blood-red eyes. Although the eastern Rufous-sided Towhee sings a clear *drink your teeeea*, the coastal towhee sings *T'weeee* or a separate, buzzy note.

Western Tanager
(*Piranga ludoviciana*)

The tropical appearance of the Western Tanager's plumage reinforces the link between the South American and west coast forests. A winter resident of the tropics and a breeder in western mixed woods, this tanager is vulnerable to deforestation at both extremes of its range.

Arriving in west coast woodlands in May, male Western Tanagers, splashed with red, yellow, and black plumage, sing robin-like songs high in the forest canopy. Often difficult to see despite their tropical wardrobe, their hiccup-like *pit-a-tik* call cascades to the forest floor, prompting a visual search.

Pileated Woodpecker
(Dryocopus pileatus)

The laughing call and rhythmic drumming of the Pileated Woodpecker echo through the stands of old growth forests. With its powerful bill and stubborn determination, our largest woodpecker chisels out rectangular cavities in its unending search for grubs and ants. These distinctive signs are often the only evidence of Pileated Woodpeckers being in a forest. These crow-sized woodpeckers are secretive and retiring birds, and seeing them is always an unexpected surprise. Watching the swooping flight and flashing white underwings, or catching a glimpse of this red-crested bird clinging to a hollow snag, are precious moments that birdwatchers seek out.

Northern Flicker

(Colaptes auratus)

The Northern Flicker is a woodpecker, but its behaviour is often more similar to a robin's. Flickers are the most terrestrial of the North American woodpeckers; they're often seen on the ground, feeding on ants or taking a dust bath. Often it is only when the Northern Flicker is around its nest cavity that it truly behaves like other woodpeckers—clinging, rattling, and drumming.

The Northern Flicker has spotty plumage, a black bib, and in flight, its white rump is distinctive. Northern Flickers on the coast have red under their wings and tails, with males having a red moustache. This coastal resident is easily seen year-round, occasionally visiting backyard feeders when snow blankets the ground.

Downy Woodpecker
(Picoides pubescens)

    This black and white bird is the smallest woodpecker and is common in wooded ravines and city parks. It's easily attracted to backyard feeders by suet (beef fat). Males are readily distinguished from females by a small patch of red feathers at the back of their heads.

    The Downy's close relative, the Hairy Woodpecker, should also be familiar. The Hairy Woodpecker is almost identical in plumage to the Downy, but it is nearly twice as large. Also, the Hairy Woodpecker's chisel-like bill is as long as its head is wide, while the Downy Woodpecker's bill is comparatively shorter.

Red-breasted Sapsucker

(Sphyrapicus ruber)

Sapsuckers have adopted a variation on the woodpecker theme: they drill lines of parallel 'wells' in tree bark. As the wells fill with sap they attract insects, and Red-breasted Sapsuckers make their rounds, collecting the trapped bugs.

Some people find the damaging effect on trees overshadows the bird's resourcefulness, but most healthy trees can withstand a series of sapsucker wells. Hummingbirds, on the other hand, enjoy the sapsucker's ability to plan in advance—so much so that they will flit by to pilfer the trapped insects while the sapsucker is away.

With its red head and red and yellow breast, this is the most colourful of North America's sapsuckers.

Black-capped Chickadee
(*Parus atricapillus*)

The Black-capped Chickadee is one of the most pleasant birds in our cities and forested areas. This exceptionally friendly bird often greets walkers along trails, welcoming them into the chickadee's world of shrubs, dry leaves, and insect eggs. Throughout most of the year, chickadees move about in loose flocks, investigating their human visitors, surrounding them with their delicate *chick-a-dee-dee-dee* calls.

During the summer, Black-capped Chickadees seem strangely absent from city parks and wooded ravines—they may be too busy raising their families to greet and entertain passersby. It seems that chickadees let flighty migrants have their way in the woods for three brief summer months, but once the first autumn chill arrives, the woods will once again be theirs.

Chestnut-backed Chickadee

(Parus rufescens)

The west coast hosts yet another bird that is the most colourful of its family. The further west and the higher in elevation one goes, the more common the Chestnut-backed Chickadee becomes. It's most common toward the islands off-shore, where it breeds.

Small bands of inquisitive birds are likely to be composed of a few Chestnut-backed Chickadees. These chickadees prefer moist coniferous forests, and are not as common within the larger cities as their Black-capped relatives. However, provided that suitable cover is nearby, Chestnut-backed Chickadees will visit backyard feeders, providing a delightful contrast with other yard guests.

Dark-eyed Junco

(*Junco hyemalis*)

While residents east of the Rockies do have Dark-eyed Juncos, only west coast residents have the splashy junco race with the black hood and tail and the chestnut body. Formerly known as the Oregon Junco, this bird has now been lumped in with its drab relatives, and they are collectively referred to as the Dark-eyed Junco.

Juncos are ground dwellers, and are frequently observed flushing along wooded trails. Although the west coast junco is relatively colourful, the trait that all juncos share— white outer tail feathers—is unmistakable when this small bird retreats. The double-scratching foraging technique and sharp, distinctive, smacking calls of the Dark-eyed Junco noisily announce the presence of this year-round resident.

Barn Swallow

(Hirundo rustica)

The graceful flight of these birds is a common sight during the summer. Barn Swallows build their cup-shaped mud nests in the eaves of barns, picnic shelters, and occasionally in nest boxes or any other structure that provides protection from the rain.

The Barn Swallow is easily recognized for its steel-blue back, chestnut throat, and long, forked tail. Swallows are insectivorous, catching flying insects in mid-flight. Because Barn Swallows are often closely associated with human structures, it is not uncommon for a nervous parent to dive repeatedly at intruders, forcing them to retreat.

Tree Swallow
(*Tachycineta bicolor*)

The population of Tree Swallows has increased during the past decades, as the unforeseen result of a bluebird nest box program. These common swallows are cavity nesters, and are among the most frequent users of nest boxes intended for bluebirds. Unlike House Sparrows and European Starlings, which are not exclusively cavity nesters and yet actively usurp nest cavities from bluebirds, Tree Swallows compete for the cavities because their own have become so scarce.

Tree Swallows and Violet-green Swallows are frequently observed spiralling around in large groups over open fields in early spring. Both are identifiable for their effortless flight and bicoloured plumage—white on the bottom and blue-green on top—but the Violet-green has a white cheek and rump. Natural flyers, swallows commonly skim low over calm water for a quick drink, leaving only a small wake behind them.

Rufous Hummingbird
(Selasphorus rufus)

You are fortunate if you are one of the few to get a prolonged look at a Rufous Hummingbird in the field. Most meetings with this west coast hummer are over before they begin—a loud hum draws attention to a small flying object flitting about, but it quickly disappears through the trees. It's often only after the bird has disappeared that its identity becomes apparent.

Fortunately, Rufous Hummingbirds are easily attracted to feeders filled with sweetened water. The male's iridescent scarlet throat and rusty body play with the sunlight in ever-switching colours. The Rufous Hummingbird's gentle appearance is misleading—these fiercely aggressive hummingbirds will chase intruders away in the energetic defence of a food source.

Red-breasted Nuthatch
(*Sitta canadensis*)

This common year-round resident of mixed-wood forests has a precarious foraging habit. Unlike other birds, which forage moving up tree trunks, nuthatches move down trunks—headfirst. They occasionally stop with their heads held out at a right angle to the trunk. By moving down the tree, Red-breasted Nuthatches are able to find seeds, insects, and nuts that have been overlooked by wood-peckers.

Although the Red-breasted Nuthatch may look like a woodpecker, its feeding habits, black eyeline, and blue-grey back should eliminate any confusion. Bird feeders in older communities adjacent to mature forests will often attract Red-breasted Nuthatches during winter. Their distinctive, nasal *yank-yank-yank* call is heard increasingly as spring arrives.

Cedar Waxwing

(Bombycilla cedrorum)

A faint, high-pitched whistle is often the first clue that waxwings are around. Search the tree tops and these cinnamon-crested birds will often serve up a pleasant visual reward as they dart out in quick bursts, snacking on flying insects.

Cedar Waxwings are most frequently seen in large flocks late in the summer, when they congregate on fruit trees and quickly eat all the berries. Cedar Waxwings are gentle; the suspicious-looking black mask does not represent this bird's inoffensive character. The Cedar Waxwing's body feathers are so fine that they are nearly indistinguishable from one another.

Common Yellowthroat

(Geothlypis trichas)

This energetic warbler of the cattails is easily identified by its looks or by its sound. The male Common Yellowthroat's oscillating *witchety-witchety-witchety* song is not easily forgotten. As this bird's name suggests, it is both common (it's the most numerous warbler in North America) and yellow-throated. The male's characteristic black mask is an unmistakable field mark.

Female yellowthroats are rarely seen because they keep their nests deep within the thick vegetation surrounding marshes. Although Common Yellowthroats are among the most common hosts of cowbird eggs, a stable and productive breeding population protects them from decline.

Yellow Warbler

(Dendroica petechia)

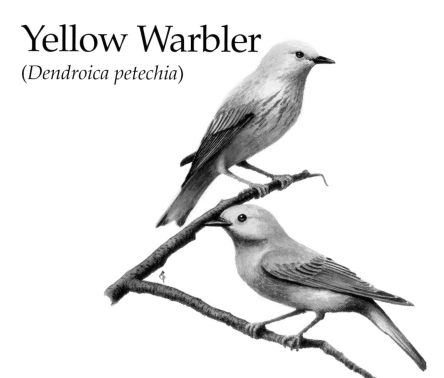

Although the Yellow Warbler is common in woodlands (especially those near water), a glimpse of one is always a sweet surprise. The male—frequently and inaccurately called a wild canary—has brilliant yellow plumage that contrasts sharply with his fine, red chest streaks.

Adding to the appeal of the Yellow Warbler is its lively *sweet-sweet-sweet-I'm-so-so-sweet* courtship song. Unlike most other species that are parasitized by cowbirds, Yellow Warblers will either abandon their nests or simply build another nest over the eggs. In true warbler fashion, the Yellow Warbler is active and in-quisitive, flitting from branch to branch in search of juicy caterpillars, aphids, and beetles.

Yellow-rumped Warbler
(Dendroica coronata)

   This spirited songbird is as common as it is delightful. Its contrasting colours, curiosity, and tinkling trill are enthusiastically admired by even the most jaded birdwatcher. The western race of the Yellow-rumped Warbler has a glorious yellow throat and was formerly called the Audubon's Warbler, distinguishing it from the eastern form. Although it no longer officially holds that title, western birders continue to refer to this spry bird by its former name, affirming its western roots and its superior attire.

   Ironically, although this warbler bore the name of one of the greatest ornithologists, it was one of the few birds that Audubon never observed. It is uplifting for some novice birdwatchers to realize that, when they see the western form of the Yellow-rumped Warbler, they are having an experience that one of the great ornithologists missed.

American Goldfinch

(Carduelis tristis)

The American Goldfinch is a bright, cheery songbird commonly seen in weedy fields, roadsides, and backyards, where it often feeds on thistle seeds. The male's black cap and wings separate it from the other yellow birds that are mistakenly called wild canaries. The American Goldfinch delays nesting until June or July to ensure a dependable source of thistles and dandelion seeds to feed its young.

The state bird of Washington, the American Goldfinch is less conspicuous during winter, because many migrate in large flocks as far south as Mexico. When it returns in late spring, the American Goldfinch swings over fields in its distinctive undulating flight, filling the air with its jubilant call, *po-ta-to-chip*.

House Finch
(*Carpodacus mexicanus*)

The male's red front end easily distinguishes the common House Finch from all other streaky brown backyard feeder birds. During the 1920s and 1930s, these birds, native to the American Southwest, were popular cage birds, sold across the continent as Hollywood Finches. Illegal releases of the caged birds, and expansion from their historic range, have resulted in two separate distributions in North America that are destined to converge.

Just as House Finches radiated out of New York in the 1940s, natural populations successfully invaded emerging cities all along the west coast, crossing into Canada in a few brief decades. As the House Finch continues to expand its range, becoming one of the most common birds in North America, it symbolizes both the intentional and indirect results of human intervention on wildlife communities.

Pacific-slope Flycatcher

(*Empidonax difficilis*)

Fortunately for birders, the Pacific-slope Flycatcher's song is much more distinctive than its plumage. When you enter any moist woodland in the spring, this flycatcher's snappy *suwheet* is one of the first identifiable sounds. If you follow this sharp song to its source, you will find a small, slim bird, patiently waiting for insects to fly into range.

Flycatchers are well named, because they often catch flying insects from a favourite perch. As they 'hawk' or 'sallie' (terms used to describe the habit of leaving a perch to snatch up a flying insect, and then quickly returning to the same perch), Pacific-slope Flycatchers can be quite entertaining.

Vaux's Swift

(Chaetura vauxi)

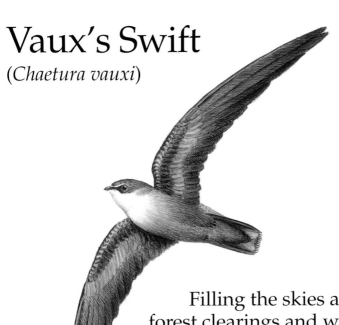

Filling the skies above forest clearings and wetlands with its gentle, twinkling voice, the Vaux's Swift spends most of its waking hours on the wing in vigilant search of flying insects.

Swifts are shaped much like swallows—long tapering wings, small bills, wide gape, and long, sleek body, but they share no close relationship. The wingbeat of swifts appears to alternate and looks uncomfortable, but it doesn't hamper the graceful flight of these aerial masters, who cast a boomerang silhouette when they glide. Swifts, when not in flight, use their small but strong claws to cling precariously to vertical surfaces. While many swifts in eastern areas choose chimneys and other structures to nest and to roost in, the western Vaux's Swift continues to prefer decaying trees for its nest area.

Golden-crowned Kinglet

(Regulus satrapa)

The high-pitched, tinkling voice of the Golden-crowned Kinglet is as familiar as the sweet smell of cedar and fir in west coast coniferous forests. Although not immediately obvious to the uninformed passerby, a birdwatcher with a keen ear, patience, and the willingness to draw down this smallest of North American songbirds with squeaks and pishes will encounter kinglets on every trip.

As these tiny birds descend in loose flocks towards the curious noise, their indistinct plumage and voice offer little excitement. It is when the flock circles about the noise, using the branches as swings and trapezes, flashing their regal crowns, that the magic of the kinglet emerges.

Brown Creeper

(Certhia americana)

The Brown Creeper may well be the most inconspicuous bird in North America. Embracing the trees of old coniferous forests, creepers often go unnoticed until a flake of bark seems to come alive. Short, purposeful, vertical hops enable the Brown Creeper to spiral up the great trunks while constantly probing the tree's wrinkled skin for hidden invertebrate treasures.

When its spiral has reached the upper branches, the tiny bird floats down to the base of a neighbouring tree to resume its grooming ascent. Only during their brief flights are Brown Creepers easily noticed, as even their thin, high-pitched whistle is too high for most birders to actually hear and rarely reveals this master of concealment.

Pine Siskin

(Carduelis pinus)

Tight flocks of these gregarious birds are frequently heard before they are seen. Their characteristic call, *zzzweeet*, starts off slowly and then climbs to a high-pitched climax. Once this distinctive call is recognized, a flurry of activity in the tree tops, showing occasional flashes of yellow, will confirm the identity of Pine Siskins.

This heavily streaked finch is subject to periodic population irruptions (volcanoes erupt, birds don't). When conditions for siskins breeding in the interior and to the north do not promote overwintering, these small birds flood into the mild coastal areas, where they readily find food in the fields and forests, and in backyard feeders.

Bushtit
(*Psaltriparus minimus*)

The character of the home reflects the quality of the occupant, and the tiny grey Bushtit sets a fine example. The architecture of its nest is worth a close look. Intricate weaving of fine fibres, spider webs, grasses, mosses, and lichens results in what you might mistake for an old grey sock hanging from a bushy shrub.

Bushtits move about in loose flocks, and delight human curiosities with their acrobatic circus. Their long tails and grey-brown plumage, though nondescript, do not hamper the identification of these curious little birds, as they often approach close enough to render binoculars unnecessary.

Song Sparrow
(*Melospiza melodia*)

What surprises are produced by this bird! The Song Sparrow's drab, heavily streaked plumage doesn't prepare you for its symphonic song. Although this common sparrow ends its tunes with a prolonged melody, it always begins with three sharp *hip-hip-hip* notes.

This year-round west coast resident is encountered in a variety of habitats. The Song Sparrow is commonly heard at dawn and dusk in city parks, backyards, and coastal forests, and the effort it expends delivering its song is commendable.

White-crowned Sparrow

(Zonotrichia leucophrys)

The White-crowned Sparrow is a bird of extremes. Its nondescript body plumage and unassuming behavioural traits contrast sharply with its unmistakable crown and its catchy song.

During early spring, these large, common sparrows are frequently heard singing their utterly distinctive phrase *I-I-I-I gotto go wee wee now* from bushes all along the west coast. A year-round resident, overwintering White-crowned Sparrows appear at backyard feeders sporadically, ensuring that each visit is viewed as a special treat to the backyard birder.

House Sparrow
(*Passer domesticus*)

This common backyard bird often confuses novice birdwatchers because it can be very nondescript. The male is relatively conspicuous—he has a black bib, grey cap, and white lines trailing down from his mouth (as though he had spilled milk on himself)—but the best field mark for the females is that there are no field marks.

House Sparrows were introduced in the 1850s to control insects. Although these familiar birds consume great quantities of insects, they have become a major pest. The House Sparrow's aggressive nature usurps many native songbirds from nesting cavities. The House Sparrow is now the most common bird in cities and farms, and is a constant reminder of human influence on natural systems.

Bewick's Wren

(Thryomanes bewickii)

This fair-weather wren follows the west coast northward but fails to reach the northern tip of Vancouver Island. In this slender distribution, the Bewick's Wren displays the classic inquisitive nature of its family. The mission in a Bewick's Wren's life appears to involve the investigation of all suspicious noises, making this bird an easy one to attract. These white-eyebrowed wrens are common in coastal towns and cities, often nesting in backyard nest boxes, wood piles, sheds, and garages—their choice limited only by their imaginations.

Winter Wren

(Troglodytes troglodytes)

This common bird of suburbs, city parks, and woodlands sings as though its lungs were bottomless. The sweet, warbling song of the Winter Wren is distinguished by its melodious tone and its uninterrupted endurance. Although this Winter Wren is far smaller than a sparrow, it offers an unending song in one breath.

Like all wrens, the Winter Wren frequently carries its short tail cocked straight up. The Winter Wren is often observed in coastal woodlands, skulking beneath the dense understorey from October to April. As spring arrives, the Winter Wren treats coastal residents to a few weeks of wonderful warbles, and then most of them leave to breed in the north.

Watching Birds

Identifying your first new bird can be so satisfying you just might become addicted to birdwatching. Luckily, birdwatching does not have to be expensive. It all hinges on how involved in this hobby you want to get. Setting up a simple backyard feeder is one easy way to get to know the birds sharing your neighbourhood, and some people find birdwatching to be simply a pleasant way to complement a nightly walk with the dog or a morning commute into work.

Many people enjoy going down to urban parks and feeding the wild birds that have become accustomed to humans. This activity provides people with intimate contact with urban-dwelling birds, but try to remember that bread and crackers aren't as healthy for birds as birdseed.

Most people who are interested in birdwatching will buy themselves a pair of binoculars. They help you identify key bird characteristics such as plumage and bill colour, and also help you identify other birders! Birdwatchers are a friendly sort, and a chat among birders is all part of the experience.

You'll use your binoculars often, so selecting a good pair is important. Choose a pair that will contribute to the quality of your birdwatching experience—they don't have to be expensive. If you need help deciding which pair would be right for you, talk to other bird-watchers, or to someone at your local nature centre. Many models are available and when shopping for binoculars, it's important to keep two things in mind: weight and magnification.

Binoculars tend to become heavy after hanging around your neck all day, so many people choose small, compact pairs, or buy thick neck straps to ease the pain in the neck. A strap that redistributes part of the weight to the lower back is also available. Reasonable magnification (7x–8x) is perhaps the best combination for all-purpose birding, because it draws you fairly close to most birds without causing too much shaking. Some shaking happens to everyone; to overcome it, rest the binoculars against a support such as a partner's shoulder or a tree.

With this simple piece of equipment and a handy field guide, anyone can enjoy birds in their area. Many birds are difficult to see because they stay hidden in the tree tops, but

you can learn their songs with the many tapes and CDs that are available. After experiencing the thrill of a couple of hard-won identifications, you will find yourself taking your binoculars on walks, drives and trips to the beach and cabin. As rewards accumulate with experience, you may find the books and photos piling up and your trips being planned just to see birds!

Keeping Bird Notes

Although most naturalists realize the usefulness of keeping accurate and concise notes of their observations, few are proud of their written records. It's easy to become overwhelmed by the excitement in the field and forget to jot down a few quick observations. It's a good idea for every level of birdwatcher to get into the habit of carrying a soft, small notebook in a large pocket or backpack. For the novice who is unsure of a bird's identity, a quick sketch (a pencil is best), and a description of the bird's behaviour and habits will help to confirm your sightings later (a simple line sketch is ideal—it really doesn't matter how artistic it is). For more experienced birders, dates and activities of an observed bird can be accumulated over time as an ongoing personal study.

A notebook also provides an excellent way to remember and relive the moment in the field at a later time. Finally, a comprehensive notebook can provide information to researchers who are looking at the dynamics of birds. Even keeping a count of feeder birds over a period of years can help ornithologists with their understanding of population ecology.

Another good way to learn about birds is to join your local natural history or bird society. You will meet many knowledgeable people who will be glad to teach you what they know about birds and to show you the best places to see them. Many organizations run field trips to some of the good birdwatching spots, and they

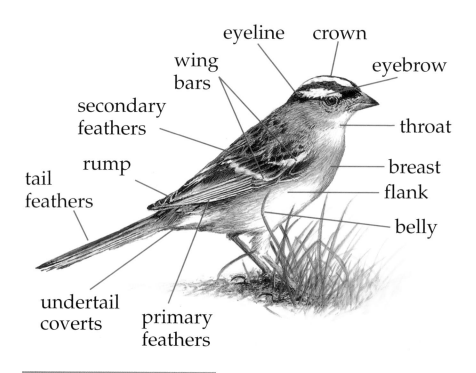

provide the benefit of an expert to help with identification problems. Christmas Bird Counts are a highlight for birdwatchers, regardless of skill level. Look for information on these in your local paper.

Bird Feeders

They're messy, costly, and they're sprouting up in neighbourhoods everywhere. Feeding birds has become a common pastime in residential communites all over North America. Although the concept is fairly straightforward (as with anything else involving birds), feeders can become quite elaborate.

The great advantage to feeding birds is that neighbourhood chickadees, jays, juncos, nuthatches and bushtits are enticed into regular visits. Don't expect birds to arrive at your feeder as soon as you set it up, it may take weeks for a few regulars to incorporate your yard into their daily routine. As the popularity of your feeder grows, the number of visiting birds will increase and more species will arrive. You will notice that your feeders will be busier during the winter months, when natural foods are less abundant. You can increase the odds of a good avian turnout by using a variety of feeders and seeds. When a number of birds habitually visits your yard, maintaining the food source becomes a responsibility because the birds may have begun to rely on your feeder as a regular source of food.

Larger birds tend to enjoy feeding on platforms, while smaller birds are comfortable on hanging seed dispensers. Certain seeds tend to attract specific birds; nature centres and wild bird supply stores are the best places to ask how to attract a favourite species. It's mainly seed eaters that are attracted to backyards—some birds have no interest in feeders. Only the most committed birdwatcher will try to attract birds that are insect eaters, berry eaters, and in some extreme cases, scavengers!

The location of the feeder may influence the amount of business it receives from the neighbourhood birds. Because birds are wild, they are wary and are unlikely to visit an area where they may come under attack. When putting up your feeder, think like a bird. A good clear view with convenient escape routes is always appreciated. Cats like bird feeders close to the ground, pouncing distance from a bush. Obviously, birds don't. Above all, a bird feeder should be in view of a favourite window, where you can sit and enjoy the rewarding interaction of your appreciative feathered guests.

Recommended Reading

Field Guides

Field Guide to the Birds of North America.
S.L. Scott, ed. National Geographic Society,
Washington, D.C.

Birds of North America: A Guide to Field Identification. Chandler S. Robbins, Bertel Brunn,
Herbert S. Zim. Golden Press, New York.

Birds of the San Juan Islands. Mark G. Lewis,
Fred A. Sharpe. The Mountaineers, Seattle.

Western Birds. Roger Tory Peterson. Houghton
Mifflin Company, Boston.

Birds of Vancouver. Robin Bovey, Wayne
Campbell. Lone Pine Publishing, Edmonton.

Birds of Victoria. Robin Bovey, Wayne Campbell,
Bryan Gates. Lone Pine Publishing,
Edmonton.

Reference Books

*The Birder's Handbook: A Field Guide to the
Natural History of North American Birds.*
P. Ehrlich, D. Dobkin, D. Wheye. Simon
and Schuster, Toronto.

The Audubon Society Master Guide to Birding.
John Farrand Jr., ed. National Audubon
Society. Knoft, New York.

The Birds of Canada. Revised edition. Earl W. Godfrey. National Museum of Natural Sciences, Ottawa.

Birds of the Pacific Northwest. Ira Gabrielson, Stanley Jewett. Dover Publications, New York.

Book of North American Birds. The Reader's Digest Association Inc., Pleasantville, New York / Montreal.

The Birds of British Columbia vols. I-IV. R. Wayne Campbell, Neil Dawe, Ian McTaggart-Cowan, John Cooper, Gary Kaiser, Michel McNall. The Royal British Columbia Museum.

Birding Magazines

Birder's World. Holland, Michigan.

Bird Watcher's Digest. Marietta, Ohio.

Wild Bird. Irving, California.

Birds of the Wild. Markham, Ontario.

Select Glossary

alcid: a group of sea birds that includes auks, murres, puffins, and guillemots

coniferous: cone-producing trees, usually softwood evergreens

corvid: a group of birds including crows, jays, and ravens

dabble: a feeding technique used by pond ducks involving submerging the head and neck to feed below the surface

deciduous: trees that lose their broad leaves annually

fledgling: the stage when young chicks acquire their first permanent feathers

foraging: feeding

hybrid: the offspring produced by the breeding of two different species

irruption: periodic mass migration of birds (usually in winter), often as a result of food shortages

migrant: a bird that nests and overwinters in different areas

ornithology: the scientific study of birds

raft: a concentration of waterbirds on open water

raptor: a bird of prey

soar: to ride air currents without flapping the wings

Index

A

B

C

Illustration Credits

Gary Ross: 23, 25, 26, 27, 28, 30, 31, 37, 39, 41, 42, 43, 44, 45, 50, 51, 52, 53, 56, 57, 62, 63, 65, 66, 67, 68, 69, 73, 74, 75, 76, 81, 83, 87, 88, 90, 91, 92, 93, 94, 97, 98, 100, 101, 103, 107, 109, 110

Ewa Pluciennik: 20, 21, 22, 24, 29, 32, 33, 34, 35, 36, 38, 40, 46, 47, 49, 54, 55, 59, 60, 61, 64, 70, 71, 72, 77, 78, 80, 82, 84, 86, 89, 95, 96, 99, 102, 104, 105, 106

Joan Johnston: 79, 85, 108

Kitty Ho: 48

Beata Kurpinski: 58

About the Author

When he's not out watching birds, frogs, or snakes, Chris Fisher researches endangered species management and wildlife interpretation in the Department of Renewable Resources at the University of Alberta. The appeal of western wildlife and wilderness has led to many travels, including frequent visits with the birds of the West Coast. By sharing his enthusiasm and passion for wild things through lectures, photographs and articles, Chris strives to foster a greater appreciation for the value of our wilderness.

LONE PINE'S FIELD GUIDES have become enormously popular for their quality and ease of use. Clear species descriptions are combined with detailed drawings and excellent colour photographs to make it easy to identify everything from towering trees to minuscule mosses. Beginners in particular will appreciate the ecosystem descriptions and the illustrated glossaries and keys. With notes on the natural history, ethnobotany, edibility, potential hazards and historical uses of plants, these guides will enhance any walk in woods and wetlands.

Plants of Southern Interior British Columbia
  by Roberta Parish, Ray Coupé and Dennis Lloyd
Over 675 species of trees, shrubs, wildflowers, grasses, ferns, mosses and lichens.
  5.5" x 8.5" • 454 pages • 1000 colour photographs
700 illustrations • Softcover • $24.95 • ISBN 1-55105-063-3

Plants of Coastal British Columbia
  by Jim Pojar and Andy MacKinnon
794 species of trees, shrubs, wildflowers, grasses, ferns, mosses and lichens.
  5.5" x 8.5" • 528 pages • 1100 colour photographs
1000 line drawings • 794 colour range maps • Softcover
  $24.95 Cdn., $19.95 US • ISBN 1-55105-042-0

Plants of Northern British Columbia
  by Andy MacKinnon, Jim Pojar and Ray Coupé
Over 500 species of trees, shrubs, wildflowers, grasses, ferns, mosses and lichens.
  5.5" x 8.5" • 352 pages • 570 colour photographs
600 illustrations • Softcover • $19.95 • ISBN 1-55105-015-3

Lone Pine Publishing
206, 10426-81 Avenue, Edmonton Alberta T6E 1X5
#202A, 1110 Seymour Street, Vancouver, B.C. V6B 3N3
16149 Redmond Way, #180 Redmond, Washington 98052
Fax: 1-800-424-7173   Phone: 1-800-661-9017